Alexander Hamilton Laidlaw

Soldier Songs and Love Songs

Alexander Hamilton Laidlaw

Soldier Songs and Love Songs

ISBN/EAN: 9783337307189

Printed in Europe, USA, Canada, Australia, Japan

Cover: Foto ©Thomas Meinert / pixelio.de

More available books at **www.hansebooks.com**

SOLDIER SONGS

AND

LOVE SONGS

BY

A. H. LAIDLAW

PRESS OF
WILLIAM R. JENKINS
NEW YORK

Dedicated

TO THE

SOLDIERS AND SAILORS

OF THE

UNITED STATES

THE TWO ARMS OF AMERICAN SALVATION

CONTENTS.

PREFACE.

In ISSUING this collection of Songs, the author makes the following acknowledgments:—

"The American *Ça ira*" was suggested while reading the French song of that name, from which song the phrase *ça ira* alone was appropriated.

In "The Song of William the Conqueror," his characteristic oath, "By the splendor of God!" is used.

In the "Death Song of the Enfants Perdus," a few remembered lines or fragments have been appropriated from an anonymous and almost forgotten English ballad.

"Burke of the Brave Brigade" was written in memory of the late Dennis F. Burke, the last commander of the Irish Brigade in the battle of Gettysburg.

"The Custer Wail" was composed in a dream, in 1877.

In the last two stanzas of "Marshall Ney's Farewell," his own language translated is used in nearly half the lines. The first line of this poem is the

expression used by Napoleon, on his voyage to St.
Helena, when sighting the shore of France for the
last time.

"The Lily Land of France" was suggested by the
French song, "Partant pour la Syrie," from which
nothing was appropriated but the accentual move-
ment.

Except in the above mentioned instances, the songs
here collected were composed without finding a model
or a suggestion in any other writer.

The "Soldier Songs" and the "Love Songs" are
printed alternately.

A. H. LAIDLAW.

SONGS

SONGS.

CUSTER.

FOILED on the field with his dead boys around him,
  All waiting for Earth to recover her own,
Fortune hath missed him, but Glory hath found him,
  While fighting a thousand fierce foemen alone.

Custer's the right wing, the left and the center,
  Himself is his only reserve and supply.
This is a battle for Spartans to enter,
  Where One makes an army to conquer or die.

Straight on his steed doth he meet the grim battle,
  The red line of danger grows deadly and large,
Loud from the hills rings the rifleman's rattle,
  But Custer is ready, so forward and charge!

Firing with left hand, and fencing with right,
  The reins in his teeth, like a handless young Hun,
What is his fate in the terrible fight?
  The thousands hath slain him, yet Custer hath won.

His foemen still seek him in terror and wonder,
  Alive in the tempest that darkens the vale;
His charge they still fear in the echoing thunder,
  His sword in the lightning, his voice in the gale.

THE AMERICAN GIRL.

THE maid for man to love,
All other forms above,
Is she whose home adorns the loam of this fair land
  of mine:
American in sire,
She's born of love and fire,
And dominates the heart of man as by a right divine.

By rhyming swain pursued,
She meets the puling dude,
Whose hopes to win are centered in his pale Platonic
  plan;
American in heart,
She spurns his petty part,
Then speeds him to the army mess to prove himself a
  man.

With tact burned in the bone,
She stands herself, alone,
The peer of peers of ancient years, for highest func-
  tions fit;
American in head,
Who woos her, she *may* wed,
If he hath grace, and wit, and worth, and sense, and
  soul and grit.

Alive. alert and sweet,
In rounded poise, complete,
Come any day what will or may, she meets the world
at par;
American in soul,
She brooks no man's control,
But brings to *one* a crystal love as stainless as a star.

Who wins, she weds, retains.
She lives, she loves, she reigns
Through home and hall, and over all the sovereign of
the scene;
American in dower,
She knows her native power,
And holds the heart of him she loves. a Woman and
a Queen.

THE GOOD SHIP "OHIO."

SWIFT o'er the lee when the wind flies free,
   Follows the ship "Ohio,"
With skies o'ercast she bends to the blast,
   Like a billowy bird she can fly, O,
And she'll leave all behind in a whispering wind
   As soft as a maiden's sigh, O.
Or when o'er the Lakes the storm-cloud breaks,
   And the waves scoop their murderous hollow,
While the weaker ship to its mooring must slip
   And safe in a harbor wallow,
In the front of the storm she fills her white form,
   And the demons of danger follow.

O for the life 'mid the storm and the strife
   Of sailor and storm and billow!
Far be my bed from the lubberly dead
   That sleep near the wailing willow,
But give me the grave of the mutinous wave
   With its heaving and whistling pillow.
Down from the skies look the spectral eyes
   Of our kelpie, sprite and bewailer,
And gathering in crowds by the shivering shrouds,
   They croon while our cheeks grow paler,
And they sing as they sweep o'er the clamorous deep:
   "We love the hot heart of a sailor!"

THE AMERICAN GIRLS.

YES! The land we love
Is a land of pretty girls,
  In grand variety;
With their many colored eyes
And their multi-colored curls,
  They'll steal thy heart from thee.

If you travel in the North,
One will gleam in glory forth,
  With her blue eyes, O, so blue!
And her flash of golden hair
Will be flirting in the air,
  While entrancing all the soul in you.
      Oho! My Boy! Oho!
Always for your weal and never for your woe,
Your little heart will gallop on the go,
  And it will not give you rest
  Within your manly breast,
Till you land yourself in toto at her toe.
      Oho! My Boy! Oho!

If you travel in the South,
You will find a rosy mouth,
  And a black eye, O so black!

And some strands of raven hair
Will purloin your heart just there,
   And you'll never get the poor thing back.
      Oho! My Boy! Oho! Etc.

If you travel in the East,
Your dear soul will have a feast
   On a sweet eye, O so sweet!
And a most seductive curl
Will there give your heart a twirl
   That will fling you at two queenly feet.
      Oho! My Boy! Oho! Etc.

If you travel in the West,
One shy glance will pierce your breast
   From a bright eye, O so bright!
And an auburn heaven of hair
Will so glorify the air,
   You'll surrender all your soul at sight.
      Oho! My Boy! Oho!
Always for your weal and never for your woe,
Your little heart will gallop on the go,
   And it will not give you rest
   Within your manly breast,
Till you land yourself in toto at her toe.
      Oho! My Boy! Oho!

Thus, the land we love
Is a land of pretty girls,
   In grand variety;
With their many colored eyes
And their multi-colored curls,
   They'll steal thy heart from thee.

THE UNION OATH.

By the Revolution's dead,
By their Blood in battle shed,
By the Earth that drank their gore,
By the Heaven in which they soar,
By the Union Stripe and Star,
By the God of Righteous War,
  Swear to conquer, or to die!
    Swear to conquer,
    Swear to conquer,
  Swear to conquer *now*, or die!

By the Revolution's dead,
By their Blood in battle shed,
By the Earth that drank their gore,
By the Heaven in which they soar,
By the Union Stripe and Star,
By the God of Righteous War,
  We will conquer now, or die!
    We will conquer!
    We will conquer!
  We will conquer *now*, or die!

BETSIE BROWN.

I HAVE loved you all my days,
    Betsie Brown,
And I'll never cease to praise
    Betsie Brown;
Still must I break love's tie,
  To act a patriot part,
But I'll yield thee, as I die,
  The last throb of my heart,
    Betsie Brown!

For my country let me die,
    Betsie Brown,
And never grieve nor cry,
    Betsie Brown,
But lay me down to sleep
  Where my country's tempests rave,
Where its mountain moss can creep
  O'er an humble patriot's grave,
    Betsie Brown!

And should my boy, with thee,
    Betsie Brown,
By my grave once bend the knee,
    Betsie Brown,

Teach him to bleed or die
For his country or his God,
Like him whose ashes lie
Beneath the loving sod,
Betsie Brown!

SWORD OF JEHOVAH.

SWORD of Jehovah, swing
O'er the world's ravening,
Wide on the tempest's wing,
   Swing far! Swing free!
Where the mailed hand is set,
Braced to the bayonet,
Bloody and warm and wet,
   Swing far! Swing free!

Strike where the sordid great
Revel in royal state,
Liberty desolate,
   Strike far! Strike free!
Where the King's coursers champ,
Where the mailed millions tramp,
Ringed round the tyrant's camp,
   Strike far! Strike free!

Fall where the Kaiser stands,
Guarded by gory bands,
Known by their bloody hands,
   Fall far! Fall free!
Till the last Despots die,
Till the Christ, lifted high,
Consummates Destiny,
   Fall far! Fall free!

BLACK EYES.

THE Blue Eye will do if the courting is through
　　And the way of the marriage is sunny,
And it helps in the fun till the sweet life is done
　　If the girl brings a mint of good money.
But when aft or before the good parson's front door,
　　With calm or a storm on the track;
For Love red, red hot, with the ducats or not,
　　There is never an eye like the Black.

The Hazel is true to you all the way through,
　　And it burns with a light warm and steady;
Only if it is Fred that she has in her head,
　　It is burning for no one but Freddie.
But the Black Eye will veer and stake kingdoms to spear
　　Whatever it likes on the track,
And as a love-lance to its lord in the dance
　　There is never an eye like the Black.

Here then is good health and without or with wealth
　　To the deep raven eye of my charmer!
It's a heavenly spell when it loves very well,
　　Only when it does not it is warmer.
And it's little I care, only so I get there,
　　Whichever I find on the track,
For Heaven or Hell in its magical spell
　　There is never an eye like the Black.

THE AMERICAN ÇA IRA.

WITH a sullen, setting Sun,
    It will come!
With the days of Despots done,
    It will come!
With a sullen, setting Sun,
With the days of Despots done,
With the wrath of God begun,
    It will come!
    It will come!

With a ruddy, bloody Moon,
    It will come!
With remorseless slaughter soon,
    It will come!
With a ruddy, bloody Moon,
With remorseless slaughter soon,
With our Tyrants stripped and strewn,
    It will come!
    It will come!

With a meteoric glare,
    It will come!
With Destruction in the air.
    It will come!

With a meteoric glare,
With Destruction in the air,
With the vengeance of Despair,
    It will come!
    It will come!

With abasement of the proud,
    It will come!
With the last King's crimson shroud,
    It will come!
With abasement of the proud,
With the last King's crimson shroud,
But with Christ within the cloud,
    It will come!
    It will come!

With the merry Morning Stars,
    It will come!
With the end of royal wars,
    It will come!
With the merry Morning Stars,
With the end of royal wars,
With the last of scourging Tsars,
    It will come!
    It will come!

Yea!   An angel from the fight,
    It will come!

With fair Liberty in light,
    It will come!
Yea! An angel from the fight,
With fair Liberty in light,
Linked with Everlasting Right,
    It will come!
    It will come!

By the Christ who hears our cries,
    It will come!
By the Spirit of the Skies,
    It will come!
By the Christ who hears our cries,
By the Spirit of the Skies,
By the God who never lies,
    It will come!
    It will come!

With a place for you and me,
    It will come!
At the feastings of the Free,
    It will come!
With a place for you and me,
At the feastings of the Free,
With eternal Jubilee,
    It will come!
    It will come!

BIRD OF THE SUMMERING NORTH.

BIRD of the summering North,
  Whither away?
Fly you so gaily forth
  Simply to stay
Nested in northern bowers
Till the late flushing flowers
Turn in October hours
  Ashen and gray?

Bear, then, this message, Dove,
  When you depart,
Safe to my northern Love,
  Quick! Like a dart!
Bill her and coo her this
Seal of triumphant bliss,
One young, immortal kiss,
  Hot from my heart.

Then, in the autumn time,
  Tailing the pole,
From my Love's cooling clime
  Make me your goal;
Flash to this field of Fame,
Linked with her darling name,
All her concordant flame,
  Deep from her soul.

THE WAR SONG OF WILLIAM THE CONQUEROR.

*"By the splendor of God!" was a characteristic oath.
of William the Conqueror.*

By the splendor of God! We come! We come!
  To fight to the death for Old England's crown,
  To reign by God's grace or in gore go down.
By the splendor of God! We come! We come!
  Sword in hand, by a King who dares
    To fight that God and our Right be made
    Our Right Divine by a bloody blade,
  Sword in hand, by a King who dares,
      By a King who dares.

By the splendor of God! We come! We come!
  In swoop for fierce flesh, like a bird of prey,
  In scent of the blood of the brave to-day,
By the splendor of God! We come! We come!
  Sword in hand, for the Love of God!
    Since blood is holy and royal wine,
    Advance! Drink health to the Norman line,
  Sword in hand, for the Love of God!
      For the Love of God!

By the splendor of God! We come! We come!
  Beware of the shock of the serried rank!
  Beware of the brand of the fiery Frank!
By the splendor of God! We come! We come!
  Sword in hand, by the Grace of God,
    We fight till death for Old England's crown,
    Till Harold, or We, with our crowns, go down,
  Sword in hand, by the Grace of God!
    By the Grace of God!

By the splendor of God! We come! We come!
  To fight to the death for Old England's crown,
  To reign by God's grace or in gore go down.
By the splendor of God! We come! We come!
  Sword in hand, by a King who dares
    To fight that God and our Right be made
    Our Right Divine by a bloody blade,
  Sword in hand, by a King who dares,
    By a King who dares!

THE LIGHT OF YOUR BEAUTIFUL EYES.

As I stroll by the stream where you stray,
   A beam is reflected afar,
Which seems, on the waters, a ray—
   The ray from a luminous star.
What is it that sweetens my sight,
   That lightens the leaf-burthened skies?
What is it, my Love, but the light,—
   The light of your beautiful eyes?

As nearer and nearer I roam,
   In the month of the rosy-mouthed June,
What is it that throws round your home
   The mirage of the mystical moon?
What is it that softens my sight,
   That mellows the marvellous skies?
What is it, my Love, but the light,—
   The light of your beautiful eyes?

As I gaze on the girl of my love,
   My ravishing, radiant one,
There seems to shower light from above,
   And I look for the summer-time sun.
What is it that dazzles my sight,
   That rivals the roseate skies?
What is it, my Love, but the light,—
   The light of your beautiful eyes?

BABYLON.

THOU art mighty,
    Babylon!
Thou art haughty,
    Babylon!
Haughty, mighty,
    Babylon!
Through thy streets the bats shall fly,
O'er thy ruins owls shall cry,
All thy chivalry shall die,
    Babylon!

Golden-godded
    Babylon!
Idol-cursèd
    Babylon!
Idol-cursèd, golden-godded,
    Babylon!
All thy gods shall bite the dust,
All thy golden godlets must
Sink to rottenness and rust,
    Babylon!

Thou art royal,
    Babylon!
Thou art ancient,
    Babylon!

Ancient, royal,
 Babylon!
Royal laws and ancient lies
Vanish when the people rise,
Truth must live, but Falsehood dies,
 Babylon!

Thou art sensual,
 Babylon!
Thou art sotted,
 Babylon!
Sotted, sensual,
 Babylon!
History this tale will tell,
To the righteous all is well;
Daniel rose, Belshazzar fell,
 Babylon!

Thou art bloody,
 Babylon!
Thou art cruel,
 Babylon!
Cruel, bloody,
 Babylon!
Cain's curse on your brow is set,
Bloodstains God will not forget,
And His curse pursues you yet,
 Babylon!

Thou art crumbled,
 Babylon!
Thou art humbled,
 Babylon!
Humbled, crumbled,
 Babylon!
Vengeance leaves no gated wall,
Vengeance leaves no gilded hall,
Vengeance blasts and buries all,
 Babylon!

THE BRITISH GYP.

THAT luscious lip, the British Gyp,
    I leave to rove, a reckless ranger,
To seek a life, with War for wife,
    Defying Death, despising danger;
Yet, while I speed from field to field,
    Enamored of the stranger's daughter,
I know the best that earth can yield
    Are nested by the British water.

Her lithe, blithe form outbraves the storm
    That spreads disaster in its shadow,
And when it clears, her form appears
    A flower upon the greening meadow;
And if, for fame, you'll have me name
    The land of most bewitching daughters,
My heart replies, with softening sighs,
    The land begirt by British waters.

Her starry eye lets arrows fly,
    That pierce the ice of arctic reason;
The kiss that thrills, the glance that kills,
    Make wild the wise and laugh at Treason;
And when, a soldier on parade,
    Beyond the bourne of British waters,
My eyes are on the stranger maid,
    My heart is with the English daughters.

DEATH SONG OF THE ENFANTS PERDUS.

'Tis here we invade the valley,
　Away from the realms of breath,
And, in most successful sally,
　We enter the gates of death;
So, stand in the last line steady,
　'Tis here our true glory lies;
Hurrah for the dead already!
　Three cheers for the next who dies!

Though here, the wet eyes of woman
　Will fill with the falling tear,
Yet, facing old Death, our foeman,
　We shout our reviving cheer.
Though high beat the hearts we cherish,
　The dead we most highly prize:
Hurrah for the first to perish!
　Three cheers for the next who dies!

The earth we now leave behind us,
　The heavens now beckon before,
Though dust of the dead may blind us,
　We march for the shining shore;
No more can our Hope deceive us,
　Our heart to it now replies,
Hurrah for the first to leave us!
　Three cheers for the next who dies!

FARE THEE WELL, O LOVE OF WOMAN!

FARE thee well, O Love of Woman!
  Lip of Beauty, fare thee well!
Thy soft heart, divinely human,
  Holds me by a magic spell.
All that grieves me now to perish
  Is the loss of one bright eye,
And I still the vision cherish
  While I lay me down to die.

At my headstone, kindly kneeling,
  May I beg a votive tear?
Woman, with her pure appealing,
  Is my angel at the bier.
Let me have but one such linger,
  Praying Christ to help and save,
Let me have but one dear finger
  Place a chaplet on my grave.

Though the soldier dies in dying,
  The true lover never dies;
Upward, from his embers flying,
  He transfigures in the skies.
Heaven is rare, but Love is rarer,
  Whether it be blest or crost;
Heaven blooms fair, but Love blooms fairer,
  But, O God, at what a cost!

Fare thee well, O Love of Woman!
  Lip of Beauty, fare thee well!
Thy soft heart, divinely human,
  Holds me by a magic spell.
All that grieves me now to perish
  Is the loss of one bright eye,
And I still the vision cherish
  While I lay me down to die.

EVER TO BE.

Ever to be
Land of the free,
Hold up your banner of light to the eye,
High!   High!
Let its folds fly,
Blessing the earth and rejoicing the sky.

Ever to be
Flag of the free,
Long as the earth shows the sight of a slave,
Wave!   Wave!
Mighty to save,
Fronting the fight in the eye of the brave.

Ever to be
Light of the free,
Lashed to the palm tree or nailed to the pine,
Shine!   Shine!
Liberty's sign,
Lighting the human to find the Divine.

JOCK AND JEAN.

JOCK.

O'ER the deep wi' me, lassie,
    Will you, will you?
Sail the sounding sea, lassie,
    Will you, will you?
Where the Sacramento flows,
'Twixt the peaks of sifted snows,
Past the fadeless Southron rose,
Sweeter than the heather-blows,
    Lassie, lassie?

JEAN.

O'er the deep wi' thee, laddie,
    Will I, will I,
Sail the sounding sea, laddie,
    Will I, will I,
Whether rivers fail or flow,
Whether roses blanch or blow,
Where thou goest, I will go,
As your loving Jean, my Jo,
    Laddie, laddie!

JOCK.

O'er the deep wi' me, lassie,
    Will you, will you?

Sail the sounding sea, lassie,
  Will you, will you?
Where the mountains, crowned with pine,
Dipping to the western brine,
Shade, with everlasting vine,
Golden grape and countless kine,
  · Lassie, lassie?

JEAN.

O'er the deep wi' thee, laddie,
  Will I, will I,
Sail the sounding sea, laddie,
  Will I, will I,
Whether mountains dip or bear
Heavenward through our future air,
Princely feast or peasant fare,
What thou darest, I will dare,
  Laddie, laddie!

JOCK.

O'er the deep wi' me, lassie,
  Will you, will you?
Sail the sounding sea, lassie,
  Will you, will you?
Where the lambies, on the braes,
Gambol in the golden haze,
And the solar disc delays
Heaven throughout the happy days,
  Lassie, lassie?

JEAN.

O'er the deep wi' thee, laddie,
　　Will I, will I,
Sail the sounding sea, laddie,
　　Will I, will I,
Wheresoe'er thy feet delay,
Drenched in rain or golden spray,
To the end of life's long day,
I will love thee as I say,
　　Laddie, laddie!

JOCK AND JEAN.

O'er the deep wi' thee, dearie,
　　Will I, will I,
Sail the sounding sea, dearie,
　　Will I, will I,
'Neath the starred or starless sky,
Heaven is where the heart beats high,
With a love that cannot die;
So we wander, you and I,
　　Dearie, dearie!

THE FLAG OF BROTHERS.

THERE is blood upon the Banner, the Banner of the
  Free,
There is blood upon *our* Banner, and it lies 'twixt you
  and me,
And, like the blood of Abel, it crieth from the sod,
And it crieth unto God throughout the Morning.

There's a blot upon the Banner, the Banner of the
  Free,
There's a blot upon *our* Banner, and it lies 'twixt you
  and me,
And, like the soul of Samuel, it riseth from the clod,
And it crieth unto God throughout the Nooning.

There's a curse upon the Banner, the Banner of the
  Free,
There's a curse upon *our* Banner, and it lies 'twixt
  you and me,
And, like the curse of Cain, it scars our brows with
  pain,
And it sears a Brother's brain throughout the E'ening.

May the Lord now bleach this Banner, the Banner of
  the Free,
And keep that Banner floating as a pledge 'twixt you
  and me,

And, like the eyes of Noah, as the Flood of Blood
    flies from us,
May we see the Bow of Promise in the Morning.

Our Banner, then, unsullied, this Banner of the Free,
Will be a Brother's Banner, held up by you and me,
And, like a Christian people, as example unto others,
We will wave the Flag of Brothers on that Morning.

WITH A HO-HO-HO! AND A HI-HI-HI!

WITH a ho-ho-ho! and a hi-hi-hi!
  With a canzonet and tabor,
Thus, with ho-ho-ho! and our hi-hi-hi!
  We amble, ramble, gambol, I
    And my lily-fingered neighbor.

With a ha-ha-ha! and a he-he-he!
  With a joyous laugh and caper,
Thus, with ha-ha-ha! and our he-he-he!
  In sunlight, moonlight, starlight, we
    Both consume our life's bright taper.

With a hi-hi-hi! and a ho-ho-ho!
  With a prancing, dancing gaiter,
Thus, with hi-hi-hi! and our ho-ho-ho!
  We ringing, singing, swinging, go,
    Through the glees of our Creator.

With a he-he-he! and a ha-ha-ha!
  Through all spells of wind or weather,
Thus, with he-he-he! and our ha-ha-ha!
  Till frailing, ailing, failing, ah!
    We will die and lie together.

Thus, with ho-ho-ho! and a hi-hi-hi!
  With a canzonet and tabor,
Yea, with ho-ho-ho! and our hi-hi-hi!
  We amble, ramble, gambol, I
    And my lily-fingered neighbor.

SEE THE FIELD OF BATTLE GLEAMS.

SEE, the field of battle gleams
Yonward past the tented streams,
    There the foe is camping;
By the thirst-assuaging rill,
From the copse behind the hill
    Hear his war-steeds champing.

Northern Knights and Southern Sons,
Onward to the gleaming guns!
    Now's the hour of battle!
Though his files be ten to one,
Seek the foe from sun to sun,
    Where his muskets rattle.

O'er the walls with slaughter wet,
O'er the ball-scarred parapet,
    Daring man and missile,
Charge to meet his best or worst,
Where his shrieking bombshells burst
    And his bullets whistle.

Roll in waves of living blue,
Pierce the columned centre through,
    Fill the world with wonder;
Rush, as with a lion's will,
Where his lightnings flash to kill
    And his cannon thunder.

Meet him with a tiger's spring,
Quicker than an eagle's wing,
    Where the bayonet piercest.
When you feel the foeman's breath,
Soldier, strike for life or death,
    Where the fight is fiercest.

Than a coward, proved and known,
Better be to atoms blown,
    Where the doomed are dying.
Welcome death in wildest way,
But to mingle with that clay
    Where the brave are lying.

Thus will Honor be our meed
For some doubly daring deed
    When we end our story.
Then in graves with roses blown,
By the hands of patriots strown,
    We will sleep in glory.

THE DYING SOLDIER TO THE NIGHTINGALE.

I PLEAD with tears to thee,
  Sweet warbler of the shade,
Breathe not such strains to me,
  The sweetest ever made.
Who bade thee slight my woes?
  Who taught to pierce my heart?
Leave me to death's repose,
  Depart, sweet bird, depart.

Still come, with every strain,
  Warm dreams of woeless days;
Still beam, on life's past plain,
  Love's long lost golden rays,
That gleam on forms gone by,
  On friends I called my own,
Who calmly rest, while I,
  Wild wandering, weep alone.

But if thou still must sing,
  Sing of my endless woes,
Of Life, a poisoned spring,
  Of Love, a scattered rose;
Wail-warble those who weep,
Wild-warble but the brave;
  To the wearied, sing of sleep,
And sing, to me, the grave.

BURKE OF THE BRAVE BRIGADE.

*Inscribed to Dennis F. Burke, last Commander of the
Irish Brigade, at Gettysburg.*

THE SPIRIT OF THE SOUTH.

" WHY come ye to this mountain, lads,
    In panoply of war?
Why leave ye the hills of your native heath,
    To seek these heights afar?"

BURKE OF THE BRAVE BRIGADE.

" We have come to unchain the slave,
    And not for a dress parade;
We have come to save man's flesh from the lash,"
    Said Burke of the Brave Brigade.
" We have heard his low cry afar,
    We have felt the self-same chain,
And we've come, my friends, through peace or war,
To make the land of the Union Star
    The land without a stain."

THE SPIRIT OF THE SOUTH.

" Go home to your native soil,
    Ye sons of the Celtic brave;
You will have to fight till the last man falls
    To free the Southern slave."

BURKE OF THE BRAVE BRIGADE.

"We have come to this fight to-day
    With no maiden, bloodless blade;
We have come to fight till the last man falls,"
    Said Burke of the Brave Brigade.
"We have felt of an iron heel,
    We have known a tyrant's hand,
We have come to fight till the Rebels reel
From the shotted shell of our cannon peal,
    And the hero-handled brand."

THE SPIRIT OF THE SOUTH.

"Then come to the battle charge!
    Welcome the Celtic yell!
'Twixt you and the South, at the cannon's mouth,
    'Tis Gettysburg or Hell!"

BURKE OF THE BRAVE BRIGADE.

"Then 'tis Gettysburg Heights or Hell!
    We are here till the game is played;
And a Hell he will feel who dares our steel,"
    Said Burke of the Brave Brigade.
So they fought, and the story runs
    (All thanks to the Heavenly Powers),
That the field was won by the Celtic sons;
For Hell flashed Leeward from out their guns,
    And Gettysburg is ours!

TEARS, TEARS.

TEARS, tears,
With wifely fears
Immixed—I held my breath,
My boy!
As down the street
The drums did beat
That led you to your death,
My boy!

Oh! Oh!
Where'er I go,
And soldier boys I see,
My jo!
I wis', I wis',
For him whose kiss
Was blessedness to me,
My jo!

Still, still,
By wish and will,
The land you saved, I love,
My boy!
Beneath a stone,
It holds your bone,
I'll clasp your soul above,
My boy!

SHERRY IN THE SADDLE.

Sherry's not in saddle,
Sherry's not in saddle,
    Zip-zip-zip! Zip-zip-zip!
    Rat-tat-tat! Rat-tat-tat!
Boys in blue skedaddle,
Boys in blue skedaddle,
    Zip-zip-zip! Zip-zip-zip!
    Rat-tat-tat! Rat-tat-tat!
Sherry's not in saddle,
Sherry's not in saddle,
    The Southron gray
    Is King to-day,
For Sherry's not in saddle.

Sherry's in the saddle,
Sherry's in the saddle,
    Zip-zip-zip! Zip-zip-zip!
    Rat-tat-tat! Rat-tat-tat!
Boys in gray skedaddle,
Boys in gray skedaddle,
    Ziz-zip-zip! Zip-zip-zip!
    Rat-tat-tat! Rat-tat-tat!
Sherry's in the saddle,
Sherry's in the saddle,

The Southron gray
Bites grass to-day,
For Sherry's in the saddle,

Sherry in the saddle,
Sherry in the saddle,
  Zip-zip-zip! Zip-zip-zip!
  Rat-tat-tat! Rat-tat-tat
Union foes skedaddle,
Union foes skedaddle,
  Zip-zip-zip! Zip-zip-zip!
  Rat-tat-tat! Rat-tat-tat!
Sherry in the saddle,
Sherry in the saddle,
  By night or day,
  'Twixt Blue and Gray,
  There's hell to pay,
When Sherry's in the saddle.

HOME! HOME!

HOME! Home!
Man may roam
While the blood of life is brimming,
While the head's with glory swimming;
But, when Love and Life are over,
Bring him to the village clover,
    Home! Home!

Home! Home!
Bring him home,
Where the songs of sad hearts shrive him,
Where remorse no more shall rive him,
Where the ever weeping willow
Moults to make its leaves his pillow,
    Home! Home!

Home! Home!
He is home,
Where his song was ever sounding,
Where his blood was ever bounding,
Here, at last, he leaves his madness,
All his love and all his sadness,
    Home! Home!

THE CUSTER WAIL.

DEAD! Where the bold and brave
Blend in one bloody grave;
Dead! With no coward clay
Weltering in gore that day.
  Dead! Dead! Ah!—Dead to me.

Dead! With his boys in blue,
Baptized in bloody dew.
Dead! Where his enemy
Fled from his fearless eye.
  Dead! Dead! Ah!—Dead to me.

Dead! Like a meteor,
Flashed o'er the field of war.
Dead! With immortal pride,
Glorious and glorified.
  Dead! Dead! Ah!—Dead to me.

Dead! Where the captives sing
Saved by his rifle's ring.
Dead! Where the painted brave
Bled by his gory glaive.
  Dead! Dead! Ah!—Dead to me.

Dead! Where the feathered game
Fell at his deadly aim.

Dead! Where the buffalo
Found him a gallant foe.
   Dead! Dead! Ah!—Dead to me.

Dead! Where the prairie steed
Vainly exerts his speed.
Dead! Where the antlered stag
Dies on the dizzy crag.
   Dead! Dead! Ah!—Dead to me.

Dead! Where the valleys sink
Low to the river's brink.
Dead! Where the mountains spring
Higher than eagle's wing.
   Dead! Dead! Ah!—Dead to me.

Dead! Where the solar glows
Eastward and upward rose.
Dead! Where the evening's gold
Westward and downward rolled.
   Dead! Dead! Ah!—Dead to me.

Dead! Where the streamy vales
Murmur their tender tales.
Dead! Where the ocean's roll
Sobs for the passing soul.
   Dead! Dead! Ah!—Dead to me.

Dead! Where the thicket's throats
Mingle their million notes.

Dead!   Where the forests dim
Tone their lone requiem.
   Dead!   Dead!   Ah!—Dead to me.

Dead!   Where the eagle's scream
Shortens the hunter's dream.
Dead!   Where the nightingale
Trills out her lonely tale.
   Dead!   Dead!   Ah!—Dead to me.

Dead!   Where no maiden fair
Weaves with his waving hair.
Dead!   Where no darling sips
Life from his loving lips.
   Dead!   Dead!   Ah!—Dead to me.

Dead!   Where no woman's breast,
Robbed of her love and rest,
Flower with a fading leaf,
Sinks in her silent grief.
   Dead!   Dead!   Ah!—Dead to me.

Dead!   Nevermore to be.
Dead!   Nevermore to be.
Dead!   Evermore to me.
Dead!   Evermore to me.
   Dead!   Dead!   Ah!—Dead to ME!

WEEP NOT FOR HIM.

WEEP not for him who, in the battle dying,
   Lives in the lays of those he sought to save;
Weep not for him who on the cold turf lying,
   Finds in his native land a patriot's grave;
Weep not for him for whom the night wind, sighing,
   Spreads o'er his bier the banner of the brave;
But, o'er the ashes of the dead hussar,
Shout to the thunder and the trump of war.

Go weep for her who, by her Love's side sighing,
   Gives to the grave the form she loved so well;
And weep for her who meets no soft replying
   To the sweet story she would die to tell;
Aye, weep for her whose Love, to Lethe flying,
   Left on her lip no mark of his farewell;
Oh, weep for her whose star of life is dim;
Weep, weep for her; but weep no more for him.

TARRY YE NOT IN EGYPT.

THE LORD is wroth with Pharaoh's men,
Tarry ye not in Egypt!
He hath raised His strong arm to smite furrow and fen,
And he'll smite them and smite them again and again.
Tarry ye not,
Tarry ye not,
Tarry ye not in Egypt!
The Lord is wroth with Pharaoh's men,
He hath raised His strong arm to smite furrow and fen,
And he'll smite them and smite them again and again,
So tarry no longer in Egypt.

The Lord hath set His sign in the sky,
Tarry ye not in Egypt!
And all the first-born in the land shall die,
The fathers shall perish, the mothers shall sigh.
Tarry ye not,
Tarry ye not,
Tarry ye not in Egypt!
The Lord hath set His sign in the sky,
And all the first-born in the land shall die;
The fathers shall perish, the mothers shall sigh,
So tarry no longer in Egypt!

The Lord hath hardened the heart of the King,
Tarry ye not in Egypt!

So the creatures that crawl and the insects that sting
Will add terror to life and bring death on the wing.
>Tarry ye not,
>Tarry ye not,
>Tarry ye not in Egypt!
The Lord hath hardened the heart of the King,
So the creatures that crawl and the insects that sting
Will add terror to life and bring death on the wing,
>So tarry no longer in Egypt!

There is blood on the river and blood on the door,
>Tarry ye not in Egypt!
The land shall be red on the sea and the shore,
And the blood of the Ruler shall reign nevermore.
>Tarry ye not,
>Tarry ye not,
>Tarry ye not in Egypt!
There is blood on the river and blood on the door,
The land shall be red on the sea and the shore,
And the blood of the Ruler shall reign nevermore,
>So tarry no longer in Egypt!

GIF A LASSIE SPURN A LADDIE.

GIF a lassie spurn a laddie
   Wi' her needless Nays,
Thraves will pet the hapless plaidie
   Wi' their loving ways;
So, if Kirsty blaw him cauldly
   As a winter day,
Bess and Belle will bless him bauldly
   Wi' the breath of May.

Prudery still affects the valley,
   Shady and alane,
Meeting souls that loveward sally,
   Icy as a stane.
On the mountain true Love singeth,
   Liberty is there;
Dalliance wingeth, Pleasure springeth,
   From her waving hair.

On the peaks abide the pleasures,
   Young and sweet and free,
Yoked with Youth's immortal treasures,
   Love and Liberty;
So, the hilltops seek whiie soaring,
   Eaglet of Love's sky;
Light adorned and Light adoring,
   Bask, and burn and die.

THE AMERICAN CONSUMMATION.

THE day of War is over
  When, to please a Prince alone,
A thousand slaughtered wretches
  Were to the eagles thrown.
There is gloom upon its glory,
  There is rust upon its sword,
For the day of Peace is dawning
  In the coming of the Lord.

Arise in Christian manhood
  And join the joyous throng,
With Jesus in your music
  And His mercy in your song;
For His blood hath been the ransom
  For the World, for you, for me,
And His love o'erflows the mountains
  In an everlasting sea.

For the Christ who rose in glory
  Shall return to earth the same,
And the warring hosts shall vanish
  At the voicing of His name;
And the stars shall flash new splendors
  At the fulness of His grace,
For the Heavens reflect His glory,
  And the Earth shall show His face.

Then, with Mercy in the mighty,
　And forgiveness in the strong,
The meek shall be our judges,
　And the Right shall rule the Wrong;
And, with one acclaim, all peoples
　Will the Love of Jesus praise,
And their Glory Hallelujahs
　Shall fill the happy days.

THE YOUNG VETS.

WE all know the face of the chap who can tell
  How he led the victorious van,
Through whose terrible yell all the enemy fell
  Or fled from this murderous man.

We all know the pate of the chap who was late,
  Too late for a wound or a scar,
A year or two late for a soldierly fate,
  And twenty too late for the war.

We all know the voice of Goliah the Great,
  Who never smelt powder, you know,
Who came to the field of battle too late
  To give little David a show.

We all know the tale of the chap who delights
  To tell all the girls he can find
Of the terrible sights, of the feuds and the fights,
  That he fought in the depths of his mind.

On a Century Map, we all know the chap
  Who can trace his proud place without fear,
Who claims the drum-tap found him first in the gap,
  Though he skulked forty miles in the rear.

MAIDEN KNICKERBOCKER AND THE GALLANT CAPTAIN PICKWICK.

MAIDEN.

O MY gallant Captain, whither and away?
Know'st thou Jersey Pirates smuggle in the bay?
Won't you take me with you for a little fly?
If the Pirates catch you, I'll shoot 'em with my eye.

CAPTAIN.

Come, Manhattan Maiden, share the sailor's pains.
If the Pirates catch me, save me from their chains.
Meantime mark the sailor mount the topmast high,
Till his trim tarpaulin almost scrapes the sky,
Luffing to the starboard, tacking o'er the bay,
Thus Manhattan Captains sail their lives away.

MAIDEN.

Who's the girl out yonder reaching up so high,
With her jack-o'-lantern darkening up the sky?
Do you think she's pretty? Do you think it pays
Standing up so bare like, with no polonaise?

CAPTAIN.

Now, Manhattan Maiden, 'tis the Law Marine
No form but that of Captain must on this Bay be seen;
So look at me, my maiden, mark my windward eye,
Neptune his sweet Venus loves no more than I.

Luffing to the starboard, tacking o'er the bay,
Thus the loving Captain sails his life away.

MAIDEN.

What are those far Highlands, blue as Beauty's eye,
Looking like the islands of an upper sky?
Take me to their summits that I may explore
All the caves and creatures I never saw before.

CAPTAIN.

'Tis a mystic saying: "He who seeks that shore
Fades and then his fate is never heard of more."
Such a distant prospect seek not now to spy,
Let one loving sailor fill your starry eye.
Luffing to the starboard, tacking o'er the Bay,
Thus the gallant Captain sails his life away.

MAIDEN.

Where is the Atlantic? I've heard grandfather say
He sailed on its huge surge from Holland far away,
O take me to the Ocean where the steamer sails,
A wonder to the lubbers and terror to the whales.

CAPTAIN.

Lubbers' yarns! My Maiden, trust you what I say,
There never was an Ocean—nothing but this Bay,
And if you'll be my bride, the whole world we'll explore,
In sight of New York Harbor and Staten Island shore.
Luffing to the starboard, tacking o'er the Bay,
Thus the married Captain sails his life away.

IT IS TIME TO BEGIN TO CONCLUDE.

YE Parsons, desirous all sinners to save,
    And to make each a prig or a prude,
If two thousand long years have not made us behave,
    It is time you began to conclude.

Ye Husbands, who wish your sweet mates to grow mum,
    And whose tongues you have never subdued,
If ten years of your reign have not made them grow
      dumb,
    It is time to begin to conclude.

Ye Matrons of men whose brown meerschaum still mars
    The sweet kiss with tobacco bedewed,
After pleading nine years, if they still puff cigars,
    It is time you began to conclude.

Ye Lawyers, who aim to reform all the land,
    And your statutes forever intrude,
If five thousand lost years have not worked as you
      planned,
    It is time to begin to conclude.

Ye Lovers, who sigh for the heart of a maid,
    And for forty-four years have pursued,
If two scores of young years have not taught you your
      trade,
    It is time you began to conclude.

Ye Doctors, who claim to cure every ill,
  And so much of mock learning exude,
If the *Comma Bacillus* still laughs at your pill,
  It is time to begin to conclude.

Ye Maidens of Fifty who lonely abide,
  Yet who heartily scout solitude,
If Jack with his whiskers is not at your side,
  It is time to begin to conclude.

Ye Spaniards, akin to the Mexican mule,
  And who have not fair Cuba subdued,
After three bloody years of your miscreant rule,
  It is time you began to conclude.

We commend to your mind Bill McKinley's big toe
  In a boot that is rugged and rude,
When that boot and that toe give you notice to go,
  It is time to begin to conclude.

Walk Spanish from Cuba, with Miles at your heel,
  And by Fitz Hugh the Southron pursued,
Or you'll learn from a thrust of American steel
  That it's time you began to conclude.

And Sigsbee will soon shoot it all very plain
  Into Blanco's most murderous brood,
That the cry from the blood of the Men of the Maine
  Makes it meet for mere talk to conclude.

MARSHAL NEY'S FAREWELL.

ADIEU to France! Land of the Brave, farewell!
  Sleep sweetly there, thy sons will watch by thee,
High as thy hills their burning blood will swell,
  To leave thee as they find thee, fair and free.
The nations gaze and tremble at thy spell,
  A vision of eternal Liberty,
Emerging from a swift and bloody birth,
The terror, wonder, glory of the earth.

Yet, France, farewell! One son may find his grave
  Beneath thy soil, and leave thee marching still,
Napoleon with his millions of the brave,
  Along the paths of glory, at thy will.
Soldiers, farewell! And when your banners wave
  Above my bones beside some nameless hill,
Stop not the thunder of your glorious tread,
To mark me sleeping with th' inglorious dead.

And farewell, Foes! Brave hearts and grand of soul;
  We fought in fierceness, now in peace we part.
My luckless heart hath ever been the goal
  Sought by your sabres, but in vain, O Heart!
Welcome to death amid the drum's far roll,
  Great souls, where I no more will dare your dart.
'Tis best to die where war's bluff banners wave,
Swathed in your guerdon, "Bravest of the brave."

Farewell, the storm-voiced Steed! the hero Horse,
    That snuffs the battle's sulphury breath afar;
The proudest form, the best compacted force,
    That hurls the earthquake on the field of war.
No more I'll ride, on his terrific course,
    That meteor maddened through the lines ajar,
While the foe, blanching at the onset, reels
Before his breath and thunder of his heels.

Farewell, volcanic din, Olympian brattle,
    The bursting bomb, the thousand-throated cheer,
Tartarean roar, the volleyed rifle rattle,
    The rocket's lightning line of fire and fear.
I sought my fate 'mid foes in brilliant battle,
    Gorging with souls the hungry atmosphere;
I find my fate from one cold coward's command,
A dozen bullets, and a friendly hand.

Thus I, once Michael Ney, Marshal of France,
    And soon a heap of dust, dishonored, sink;—
I, who have vanned the Empire's fierce advance
    In triple continents of fame to drink,
And bore its backward but still levelled lance
    From Borodino to the icy brink
Of Beresina; thence defiance hurled
To the linked thunders of th' embattled world.

No bandage bring.   Stark-eyed the hero dies.
    Do you not know that thus for twenty years

I've faced both ball and bullet!—for no prize
    But weal of France, my country? In man's ears,
Yea, and before God's all-beholding eyes,
    I swear I never wronged her. But Death nears.
Marshal no more, behold a man expire!
So now, make ready! Aim! Dear comrades, fire!

THE LILY LAND OF FRANCE.

WITH pensive memories
　We part the Ocean foam,
To find 'neath summer skies
　A country and a home.
O lily land of France,
　Farewell! Farewell, Paris! (*Pa-ree*)
Farewell to Life's romance!
　Welcome the sounding sea!

Soon, soon, our fading forms
　Recede into the sea,
Which, dark with all its storms,
　Will veil our hearts from thee.
O lily land of France,
　Farewell! Farewell, Paris!
Farewell to Life's romance!
　Welcome the sounding sea!

In vain, in farther climes,
　Athwart the sweeping sea,
We seek, in other times,
　The heaven we've lost in thee.
O lily land of France,
　Farewell! Farewell, Paris!
Farewell to Life's romance!
　Welcome the sounding sea!

THE THREE P'S.

THE PRATIE, THE PIG AND POTEEN.

'TIS daily this baste
    Will prosade to the fayste,
The best that Ould Oireland has seen;
    The P's are but three,
    But they're plenty for me,—
The Pratie, the Pig, the Poteen.

The Pratie, in place,
    Has an iligant face,
That my mouth opens wide to let in,
    But, like Widow Machree,
    He's so glad to see me,
That he laughs himself out of his shkin.
    He's so round and so square,
    As he laughs at me there,
That he looks loike my brother, I ween;
    Then I put him to cool
    On the top of a shtool,
Till I take a wee drop of Poteen.
    Then I put him to cool
    On the top of a shtool,
Till I take a wee drop of Poteen.

But gourmands, ahoy!
The Pig is the Boy!
Indade he's the girl to my taste;
The form is so nate,
The lip is so swate,
That I kape her quite close to my waist.
But no cannibal I,
When I look in her eye,
The loikes to my sister is seen;
So I piously pause
In the work of my jaws,
Till I take a wee drop of Poteen.
So I piously pause
In the work of my jaws,
Till I take a wee drop of Poteen.

Lave the Pratie to cool
On the top of the shtool,
While we master this question of shtate,
Shall I ate?   Shall I swig?
Musht Poteen or the Pig
Be the first or the last on my plate?
Now my grandfather's ghost
Appears at this post,
So solemn, so awful in mien,
To assist and debate
This question of shtate
On the subject of Pork and Poteen.

So he called for his mug,
And I gave him the jug,
Which he placed at his delicate mouth,
And he drank it all down,
Down, down, Derry down,
He had such a terrible drouth.
Then, with jug held on high,
And Poteen in his eye,
He says—this good ghost says to me:
"Hist! Hist! Patrick, hist!
And hould ye your whist
While I shpake out this Scripture to thee.

'Tis Hibernian Law
That, for Oireland's ould jaw,
If, at pig-faystes, you ate, shpake or swig,
If you have a great mind,
You surely will find
The Poteen's the best part of the Pig.
'Tis Hibernian Law
That, for Oireland's ould jaw,
If, at pig-faystes, you ate, shpake or swig,
If you have a great mind,
You surely will find
The Poteen's the best part of the Pig."

So, since that great day,—
Or that night I may say,—

I cook nothing else for to ate;
    By the hole o' my coat,
    It bates Houlahan's goat
In putting Pat off of his fate.
    So, for Erin go bragh,
    'Tis both Gospel and Law
For to ate, or to shpake or to swig,
    If you have a.great mind,
    You surely will find
The Poteen's the best part of the pig!
The Poteen's the best part of the pig!